I0478782

UNLOCKING THE M CUBE

How to Master the Six Sides of Small Business Success

FRANK FELKER

POWER HOUSE PUBLISHING

ALEXANDRIA
VIRGINIA

Unlocking The M Cube

How to master the six sides of small business success

by Frank Felker

Published by:
Powerhouse Publishing
625 N. Washington Street, Suite 425
Alexandria, Virginia 22314

info@powerhousepublishing.net
703-982-0984

Copyright ©2017 Frank Felker

All rights reserved. No part of this book may be reproduced in any form or by any means electronic or mechanical including but not limited to photocopying, recording, or by any information storage and retrieval system without written permission from the authors except for the inclusion of brief quotations in a review.

First Paperback Edition June 2017

Frank Felker
Unlocking the M cube, how to master the six sides of small business success

Cube icon over graphic: Copyright 2017 Digital Media Positioning, LLC. Produced as a work-for-hire by CD Studio, Bosnia-Herzegovina

Cover background image: Bigstock. Used under license.

Regarding interior photos and illustrations: every effort has been made to identify the creators and secure use permission. If you are aware of a image in this book which you believe is being used without permission contact the publisher immediately.

Table of Contents

Dedication

This book is gratefully dedicated to my sweet, loving mother, Phyllis Sally Tobias "Toby" Felker.

Toby had an adventurous spirit and a never-say-die attitude which led her to start a small business at a time when she was freshly divorced and raising a teenage son as a single parent. She had no capital, no plan and no experience - neither in business in general nor in the industry she was entering. But what the heck? The Lord is my shepherd; I shall not want.

She and I spent over 20 years figuring it out together, building the firm she started from scratch into a company that eventually produced over $1 million in annual sales.

My mother was famous for her many Tobyisms but one of her favorite sayings was Psalms 118:24:

Today is the day the Lord hath made. Let us rejoice and be glad in it.

Her unflagging optimism was an inspiration to every person she met. She continues to inspire me every day.

Thank you for everything Mom. You will never be forgotten.

Preface

My entrepreneurial journey began February 24, 1972. That was the day my mother, Toby Felker, opened a copy shop on Backlick Road in Springfield, Virginia, named Copy Right.

Toby decided that what Springfield needed was "a store that sells copies." This was about 18 months after Kinko's first opened in Santa Barbara, California, so it was a good idea at just the right time. Unfortunately, neither she, with absolutely zero business experience, nor I, a 13 year-old pain-in-the-neck boy, knew anything about business. And trying to earn a living 10¢ at a time is a hard way to go.

I don't have a photo of our original location, occupying 100 square feet in the front window of a storefront-based job printing company, but this is our shop 20 years later. It doesn't look like much, but it was a veritable palace compared to what we started with.

Here it is in all its glory; two thousand square feet of side-by-side storefronts. By the time this picture was taken, we were generating hundreds of thousands of dollars per year in top line revenue and making a good living. But it wasn't always that way.

For almost ten years the shop didn't make any money. We weren't broke, we were poor. I don't remember ever going hungry, but we were literally scraping by week-to-week, month-to-month. I was too young to be involved in the family finances but as I look back on it now I have no idea how Toby was paying the mortgage and utility bills.

The best illustration I can think of to demonstrate our difficult financial situation is this 1976 Chevrolet Chevette. The car itself, which was later named one of the *Top 50 Worst Cars Ever*

Manufactured, and the story of how we came to own it, perfectly epitomize how badly our little shop was failing.

The Chevette was just awful. It had no side view mirror on the passenger side, no radio and no back seat. I can tell you, as a young man, this was not exactly the hippest ride in town. I got a lot of good-natured ribbing from my friends about it and once came out a house party to find it laying on its side next to the curb. But, if it weren't for that car we would have had no car at all.

1976 Chevrolet Chevette

And we would not have even had the Chevette except for the generosity of the local Chevrolet dealer, Mike Pallone. Mike's wife Armeda, who was one of my mother's biggest fans, browbeat her husband until he agreed to co-sign a car loan for Toby. Of all the cars on his lot, he chose the very cheapest one – minimizing his downside risk. Clearly Mike Pallone understood how to protect his profits.

But it wasn't being poor that really bothered me, it was being ignorant.

I like to count myself as a smart person and so could not bear, time after time after time, not understanding what was going on with our small business and with the other small businesses that we were dealing with. Pricing, competition, marketing, cash flow, bookkeeping – you name it, I didn't understand it. I was angry, frustrated and deeply ashamed.

So, as Scarlett O'Hara did in *Gone With the Wind*, I made a promise to myself that, "As God is my witness, I will never be ignorant again." I made it my life's purpose to understand entrepreneurship and have spent the last 45+ years observing, analyzing and recording what differentiates the small fraction of business owners who thrive and succeed from the vast majority who struggle and fail.

Though I have founded and run many businesses since we sold the shop in 1995, none have offered a better perch than that little store to observe a wide gamut of industries and meet people from every walk of life. At that time the local copy shop / print shop was like the corner barbershop for small business owners. Everyone came there to get their forms, business cards and flyers, sharing stories and gossip over the counter while they waited.

Early on I noticed that most business owners were struggling like my mother and I. (Well, perhaps not as badly as us but struggling nonetheless.) And yet there were a small number of successful business owners who rolled up to our shop in Cadillacs and sports cars, who bought $300,000 motorhomes, sent their kids to private schools and took their families on European vacations. These people were almost like local royalty among the small business community.

I wanted to know what made them different from the rest of us. Were they just plain smarter than others? Had they won the genetic lottery, born with the "Entrepreneurial Gene?" Had they inherited money or been handed the family business? What was it? I have spent decades closely observing thousands of small business owners across the country in a single-minded quest to answer those questions.

What I've found is that there are six primary areas of focus – all of which begin with the letter M – that successful business owners master in the correct sequence, and unsuccessful business owners do not.

This successful M Cube sequence is the key to unlocking your business success:

1. Mission
2. Marketing
3. Money
4. Machine
5. Management
6. Minutiae

I Love Entrepreneurs

As you read this book you may sometimes get the impression that I am being a little harsh on my fellow small business owners. If I am, it is due to that most human reaction of becoming supremely irritated when watching others make your same mistakes.

I love entrepreneurs - all you crazy risk takers, hard workers, dreamers of dreams and solvers of problems. No matter what level of success you are currently experiencing, I know you are out there working your tails off.

Entrepreneurship is one of the highest forms of service one can perform in private industry and I believe that, when practiced correctly, it can solve most of the world's problems, one successful life at a time.

The bottom line is this: Toby and I suffered for years due to our own ignorance and lack of marketing knowledge or implementation. Since then I have witnessed scores of other individuals, couples and families endure similar financial and emotional hardships due to poorly planned and ultimately unsuccessful small business ventures. I don't want you to be one of those people.

I am giving you the straight, unvarnished truth in an effort to open your eyes to what you are really getting yourself into. Rest assured that I am offering you these words from a place of love and a desire that you achieve all of your dreams.

Here's to your success.

Author's Note:

The short book you are reading was taken from the transcript of a 10-minute presentation I gave on the topic to BNI Positive Power in Alexandria, Virginia on February 15, 2017.

I will also be writing individual eBook titles that explain each of the 6 Ms in greater detail.

Once all seven books are completed, they will be compiled into a single comprehensive title which will be published as an eBook, in paperback and hardcover print editions and as an audiobook.

All of this information will also be published as an online course at YourSchoolOfSmallBusiness. com.

Introduction:
The Definition of Success

The purpose of this book is to give you a glimpse into what is required for one to succeed as the owner of a small business. But what, exactly, constitutes successful business ownership?

A successful business is one that

- Funds your dream life
- Allows you to work fewer hours while
- Making you more money than you would at a similar job you're qualified for
- And then, ultimately, is an asset you're able to sell for a big balloon payout

You've probably heard the line that about 80% of all businesses fail after five years. I have no idea where that statistic comes from, because when I look at the data, I see a 99% failure rate.

According to Forbes.com, 543,000 businesses are founded in the US every month on average. That works out to over 6.5 million annually. But the website BizBuySell.com, reports that only 7,842 U.S. businesses were sold in 2016, according to transactions reported to them by business brokers nationwide. Based upon the fourth criterion I listed above, that's a failure rate of over 99%.

And what is a "Dream Life?" Whether that is 2.5 kids and a white picket fence or the laptop lifestyle in a Tahitian hammock is up to you. Whatever it is, I'm willing to bet it is NOT working 80-hour weeks pulling your hair out, wondering how you're going to pay the rent. Small businesses that are still operating but causing their owners nothing but heartache are not successes. Statistically, however, they won't be counted as "failures" until they finally and painfully close their doors.

Why Start A Business?

People start businesses for a wide of variety reasons and at every stage of life. There is the discontented creative person who leaves their six-figure corporate job to spend more time with their family and do something they have a burning passion for. (Listen to my interview with Brian Anderson, founder of Valhalla Bladeworks, on the *Radio Free Enterprise* podcast).

Boomerpreneurs confront retirement by refusing to spend the rest of their lives in a rocking chair or "staying active" by greeting customers at the local Wal-Mart. Their kids are grown. Their homes are paid for. They have decades of business experience, a big nest egg and plenty of gas left in the tank. Starting "a little business" sounds the like perfect course of action. My counsel to Boomerpreneurs is to move slowly, very slowly. If their temperament were truly entrepreneurial they would have started a business of some kind many years ago. And it only takes one bad business venture to quickly burn through your entire nest egg and leave you deeply in debt.

Vetrepreneurs leave military service with incredible leadership skills, laser-sharp mission focus and a level of work ethic that makes it look like their life – and the lives of everyone around them – depends upon the successful completion of a given task. (watch my *Semper Startup 2014 Opening Remarks* on YouTube). But the transition from active duty military service to civilian life is difficult enough without adding the small business learning curve to the mix – especially for people for whom failure can literally feel like death. And understanding that business, unlike warfare, is not a zero-sum game, can be hard to accept.

Because of the wide variety of mindsets and objectives of prospective business owners, my definition of success may not match yours. But I'd like to share a few things you should keep in mind when formulating your own definition.

It Has To Beat Working For The Man

A successful business owner is working fewer hours for more money than best-paying job their resume would allow for in the labor market. The only caveat to that rule is if you are so miserable at your "real job" that would do almost anything to escape it. Keep in mind however that escapism doesn't put food on your family's table or a roof over their heads. That's why they call it work.

If you were working 50-60 hours per week for a great salary at a stable company, with three weeks of paid time off, employer contribution to a retirement plan and participation in a group health plan, but are now working 80-100 hours per week in your business for half the pay, no benefits and no vacation in sight, you should have never quit your job.

You Must Be Paid Three Ways

As a business owner, you should really be making money three ways: as an employee; as a lender; and as an owner/stockholder. If you're not generating better returns within your business for the money and time you are investing you are a 99 percenter (read Failure).

You could have left your nest egg in your retirement account, left the equity in your home, left the cash in your savings account. But you didn't. You put it all at risk to fund your business venture. If the returns those investments are generating from your business are not in alignment with the high level of risk you have put them at, you are not a wise investor.

The Ongoing Cash Generating Machine

After your first 18-24 months in business you should have more time and money freedom than you had before you started. If you don't, in my opinion, you have failed. Your business venture is a dead man walking and you're the one leading the parade.

The Big Balloon Payout at The End

As I will explain in M1: Mission, you must begin with the end in mind. In addition to generating a great income and lifestyle for yourself and your family while you run the business, you must be focused on building an asset that you can sell when you decide the time has come to move on. Venture capitalists refer to this as a "Liquidity Event."

Selling a business for the right price is not easy but it becomes much easier if you have been focused on a successful transaction from day one. Build your Book. Create an operations manual for your business that covers everything that needs to happen from when the lights are turned on in the morning until they are turned off at night. The McDonald brothers had done just that, making Ray Kroc's job of selling not one but thousands of McDonald's franchise restaurants a much simpler proposition.

The M Cube
Explained

Author's Note:

I will begin this book with M2: Marketing, then go through Ms 3-6 before ending with M1: Mission.

There are a number of reasons I am taking this approach.

- Marketing was the first clear differentiator that appeared to me.
- I still see Marketing as the single most important success factor, the only one that can single-handedly power a small business to success.
- Mission was the last area of mastery that was revealed to me.
- Mission is all about you. The other 5 Ms are about your business.

I believe you will see the method in the madness of this approach once you have finished reading this book.

M2: Marketing

The single biggest difference between the 99% of businesses that fail and the 1% that succeed is Marketing. Business owners that succeed understand and implement marketing on a consistent basis. Business owners that fail do not.

No Sales=No Business

How many times have you heard someone say "I have a great idea for a business!"? It may actually be a great idea, but until you try to convince someone to spend real money for it you'll never know.

The marketplace is the arbiter of what is and what is not valuable. Why does a teacher with an advanced degree earn $35,000 per year while a famous actor or athlete with a bad attitude and very little in the way of brain matter makes $35 million? Better marketing.

When Apple introduced the Macintosh operating system in 1984 it was a revelation, clearly superior to Microsoft DOS or even Windows 3.1, which came out nine years later. So how did Microsoft gain 93% market share and surpass Apple's revenue levels by two orders of magnitude? Better marketing.

Here's what I'm driving at: If people aren't buying what you're selling you're not in business. And that is almost certainly because your marketing - not your product or service - sucks.

Most People Hate Marketing

The problem is, you don't want to be perceived as "a salesman." You hate the idea of being self-promotional and so start a retail business believing that if you build it they will come. I know that's why I spent many years behind the counter of the print shop waiting for people to walk in rather than going out into the community and selling my wares as my more successful competitors did.

I've seen people who had every conceivable opportunity to succeed—money in the bank, decades of industry experience, you name it—but they couldn't sell their way out of a paper bag, and failed.

I've seen other people who not only didn't know how they were going to fulfill their promises, they weren't even quite sure *what they were promising*. But they still were able to sell, bring in cash, fund their business, fake it 'til they make it, and succeed.

As a business owner, if you are unwilling to be self-promotional or do sales and marketing, I suggest you get into some other line of work, because small business success is not going to happen for you.

[For a great explanation of how Groupon created a multi-billion dollar company by exploiting small business owners' fear and distaste for marketing, see my video *The Groupon Conundrum* on YouTube]

Build a Customer Factory

For many years, starting late in my print shop days, I tried to sell marketing products and services to small business owners. I found it difficult to sell people something they didn't want and so moved on to other ventures.

If you are one of those people who doesn't like marketing, but would still like to succeed in business, I suggest you sign up for my course *"How to Build a Customer Factory"* on Udemy.

M3: Money

Money Is a Tool. Handle It.

The next thing I learned about successful people is that they do a better job handling money. They understand it. They use it as a tool. They don't see solely as the ultimate goal, but also the life blood of their business.

When you have no money in the bank, your business is insolvent. You may have tens or hundreds of thousands in Accounts Receivable or other "assets" out there somewhere but if your biggest supplier is dropping a C.O.D. delivery of critical materials this morning, and you have to write a bad check to cover it, you're in trouble.

Successful business owners don't let this happen. They understand that profit is a matter of opinion but cash flow is a matter of fact. They budget and schedule the money flowing in and out. They secure lines of credit to smooth out the ups and downs. They don't allow themselves to be stretched too thin – even if it means letting a potential "big opportunity" pass them by. They manage risk as well as they manage money.

Price for Profit and Keep Costs Low

While it is only a matter of opinion, profit is an important concept nonetheless. In short, it is the primary object of owning a small business. If you are not consistently generating a profit you are engaging in what my dear old Dad used to call "An exercise in futility."

But how does one generate a profit? By keeping costs lower than revenues.

Let's Start with Revenues

A bad salesperson will deeply discount a price in order to close a sale. They believe, incorrectly, that price is the number one consideration on the mind of the buyer, when in fact perceived value is the most important variable.

As a business owner, you must price for profit. And in order to make that higher price stick you have to clearly communicate the value proposition of your product or service and why it is superior to your competitors'. All of that is a marketing function. If it doesn't translate into prices you can profit from you need to drop back to M2.

Why Cutting Costs Counts

Benjamin Franklin once said that a penny saved is a penny earned. Here's what that means to small business owners.

Let's say that you sell $100 worth of widgets and your profit margin is 10%. You have increased your sales by one hundred dollars (yay!) but you have only "earned" ten dollars (boo!).

But if you are able to find a way to cut costs by $100, every bit of that flows right to your bottom line. The hundred dollars saved is a hundred dollars earned.

The fastest way to save is to find the biggest numbers on your income statement and come up with creative ways to cut them deeply – like 15% - 25% or more. If you have employees, then labor is doubtless going to be one of your biggest expense categories. I learned in the printing business that almost every dollar I saved on labor dropped right into my pocket. That means sometimes you have to let one or more people go – one of the most difficult tasks you'll ever face.

Successful business owners are notoriously thrifty. Understanding Franklin's edict, they see every dollar saved as one dollar closer to their next European vacation, year of college tuition, fancy automobile – or whatever it is that motivates them personally. Cutting costs in order to meet your goals is tough. Business ownership is not for the faint of heart.

Accounting Literacy

If you can't read, you are illiterate. If you can't read financial statements, you are accounting illiterate. People who succeed are accounting literate. They understand what their balance sheet is telling them. They understand what their income statement is telling them. This is an enormous differentiator between those who succeed and those who don't.

Simply stated, your balance sheet tells you how your company is doing today and your income statement tells you how it has been doing over a given period of time, usually the most recent month, quarter or year. Successful business owners know which numbers and ratios are the most meaningful on those statements and they focus their day-to-day actions and decisions on achieving those outcomes.

If trying to read financial statements gives you a headache, I feel your pain. In spite of having a degree in Economics and years of business ownership experience, I never really understood what I was looking at until I took a one-day course called Color Accounting. The result was relief, surprise and empowerment.

You can learn more about Color Accounting by listening to *Peter Frampton Teaches Color Accounting* on the *Radio Free Enterprise* podcast, available on the iTunes Store. [No, he's not that Peter Frampton] You may also want to visit ColorAccounting.com and sign-up for their weekly email newsletter.

M4: Machine

In the parlance of The M Cube, Machine refers to the nuts and bolts of your business – the printing, baking, repairing, landscaping, advising, etc. that you do to generate revenue. You can be forgiven for thinking this is the number-one priority for running a successful business but, in fact, it comes in fourth place in terms of startup success factors.

The E Myth

Every current or prospective small business owner needs to read Michael Gerber's seminal book on entrepreneurship, *The E Myth*. In it, Gerber states that the belief that all small business owners are entrepreneurs is a myth. Most instead fall into two other categories he refers to as Technicians and Managers.

Technicians cut the hair and turn the wrenches. Managers know how to hire and manage technicians and generally keep the Machine of the business operating smoothly. Entrepreneurs know how to start or buy profitable businesses and hire and retain great managers.

Which one of these hats do you prefer to wear?

People who go into business often choose an industry they have a technical aptitude for, or that they have some professional experience with. Two examples are an automobile mechanic who decides to open a repair shop, or a hairdresser who decides to open a salon.

What they quickly discover is that operating an auto shop or running a salon is an entirely different thing than cutting hair or turning wrenches. Your success or aptitude in one has absolutely no bearing upon your success or aptitude in the other.

True entrepreneurs can move from owning one type of business to another, even without technical knowledge of the services provided. That's why Machine comes in fourth place behind Mission, Marketing and Money.

If you prefer the manager or technician hat, you might be able to make more money in fewer hours with less stress and at a lower risk factor by working for someone else. If you absolutely cannot bear the thought of returning to a J-O-B, then all the money you're leaving on the table and the extra stress you're eating is the price of your independence.

M5: Management

When people ask for my help with hiring someone I ask, "Have you already hired them?" If they say, "No," then I tell them, "Don't. People are hard to deal with." And every person you hire today is someone you may have to fire somewhere down the line. No fun there.

In my video, *How To Hire Great People With Craigslist* (available on YouTube), I go into a detailed explanation of the mistakes most small business owners make when it comes to hiring and managing people. I will return to that level of detail when I write an entire book on M5: Management in the near future.

For now, suffice it to say that hiring people is one of the last things you should be considering doing. That's why it's number five on my list. It is also why our entire economy is turning away from 40-hour weeks, W-2 jobs and cradle-to-grave employment relationships.

The Surplus Value of Labor

Karl Marx (the founder of Communism) came up with a concept he called the Surplus Value of Labor, which he used to describe how Capitalists squeeze value out of employees. In his view, charging a customer more for a laborer's efforts than what the laborer earned was exploitation. Maybe so, but that's what makes the business world go 'round.

If you can't hire somebody for $10 and sell their services for $20 or $30 or $100, you're in trouble. And if you're paying them for 40 hours per week but are only able to bill for 20, it's never going to work. Outsource, contract, sub-contract, do it yourself – do something, anything – but don't hire someone to perform a task until you can consistently bill many times more for their services than you're paying.

Hire and Manage Systematically

If you're still sure you need to hire someone then for goodness' sake, do it systematically. Start with an assessment of your own skills, experience and temperament. Are you the X Style Manager who announces "The beatings will continue until morale improves" or the Y Style Manager who leads by example and gives his people every opportunity to succeed?

Either way you need a system to support your style. Start with a clear job description that outlines duties and responsibilities. Make sure you give people the authority to make decisions – and mistakes – that is in alignment with their level of responsibility. Make it clear what success looks like, to whom they report, when their performance will be evaluated and based upon what criteria.

Use mistakes as learning opportunities and realize that you cannot coach integrity, intelligence or energy so you have to hire for them instead. Write employment ads that speak directly one-to-one from you to an avatar of the perfect candidate.

I will go into greater detail on this topic in the upcoming book M5: Management. In the meantime, please watch the video mentioned above.

Hire Like Coach K

Duke University basketball coach Mike Krzyzewski only hires assistant coaches whose passion and goal is to become head coach of their own team. While they are on his staff he does everything that he can to help them learn their craft and grow as leaders. He shares every secret and offers every support, even knowing that they will only be with him a short period of time.

Why does he do that? First, because it allows him to attract the very best coaching talent, which in turn helps him attract the best players.

Next, like all wise souls, Coach K understands that all relationships are temporary so you need to make the best of your partnership while you can and then bless the other person on their way out of your life.

While they're with him, these itinerant coaches work hard and win. And Coach K just keeps rolling on as the Genius of Cameron Indoor Stadium.

Do the same. Hire people who are smart, honest, ambitious and of high integrity. Find out what is important to them in their lives and then do everything in your power to help them achieve their goals. They in turn will do nothing but make you look great every day they're with you.

M6: Minutiae

Minutiae (pronounced min-NOO-sha) is a noun that refers to minute and trivial details. Here's how it applies to you.

Start-up business owners often sabotage themselves by thinking they can't move forward until they have their corporate structure set up, insurance policies in place, a business license, flashy website, etc. You can spend tens of thousands of dollars on these details and still fail. They can't help you if nobody's buying what you're selling and/or you don't have any money in the bank.

Some business owners busy themselves with these tasks in order to avoid facing their fears about Ms 2-5. While your girlfriend may be impressed that you've created a sub-chapter S corporation and have a pile of fancy new business cards, that ain't going to cut it out in the marketplace. If you want to prove you're in business, go out and sell something.

Of course, all of those things become important over time. You must have them in place in order to assure your long-term viability in business. They just won't support your initial success, which is what this book is about.

M1: Mission

I saved the best for last.

I have met many entrepreneurs who were making a lot of money but did not meet my definition of success. They were working 80+ hours per week, had no family life, screamed at their employees and chugged Pepto-Bismol to keep the acid reflux at bay. A competing print shop owner who built and sold his multimillion-dollar shop comes to mind as a perfect example of this outcome.

I also have met many entrepreneurs who achieved an excellent work-life balance, even knowing that time spent away from work would mean lost revenue and profits. Nevertheless they made an excellent living while minimizing risk and business travel. They created their dream life. A long-time friend in the training industry immediately comes to mind in this case, as does a young man who once worked for me in the printing business and went on to build a large trade show exhibit company in the small town where he went to college.

For you to achieve your definition of success you need to get right down to the roots of your motivation. Why did you decide to start a business in the first place? To support your family? Fund your retirement? Pay for college? Buy a boat?

Whatever it is, getting clear about your "Why" will help you power through every obstacle you come up against.

Mean Business, Serious Business

There is a famous scene from Godfather II where Salvatore Tessio, played by Abe Vigoda, is about to be taken for a ride because of his disloyalty to Michael Corleone. "Tell Mike it was nothing personal," Tessio tells Tom Hagen, played by Robert Duvall, "It was only business." To which Hagen replies, "He understands that Sally."

The rules of engagement in business are different than in the relationships among friends or family members, which is why I recommend you never hire nor do business with either. People must be held to account, agreements must be kept, bills have to be paid, people get fired and sometimes you even have to sue someone.

If you are not ready, willing and able to occasionally put on your tough guy face, tell people things they don't want to hear and endure difficult situations and conversations, you may not want to go into business. The benefits of successful business ownership also can incite jealousy and greed. Competitors want to come storm your castle. You must be emotionally prepared.

This is one reason why business ownership is more difficult for women than men. It's not because they don't have the guts – anyone who thinks that female is the weaker sex is an idiot. It's because a woman who puts on the tough guy face risks being called a bitch, while a man – who may be equally disliked – is still seen as strong and powerful.

If you don't mean business, serious business, you won't succeed.

Be Clear on Your Why

I have touched on this topic a number of times but feel it deserves further exploration.

I recently ran a survey of Baby Boomers (born 1946-1964) asking their responses to a variety of questions regarding the idea of starting a business in retirement.

Here's what they had to say on the question of why they were considering such a move.

Staying busy / mentally active	78%
Staying engaged with other people	67%
Supplementing retirement income	67%
Generating extraordinary income levels	44%
Desire to do something completely new and different from your past career	39%
Identify yourself as an entrepreneur / innovator / business owner	28%
You have a BIG IDEA you want to bring to life	28%
Building a legacy to pass on to children / grandchildren	22%
Show what you can do / prove yourself to a boss, parent, sibling or spouse	11%

(The percentages don't total to 100% because respondents were able to choose all answers that applied to their thoughts.)

We all need to choose a business which is going to support our "Why". If all you're looking for is something to keep you busy and engaged with society, don't drop $500,000 on a big franchise. Conversely, if you're interested in generating extraordinary income levels you're either going to have a lot of money to invest or a patent on the next big idea in your pocket.

Not having a clear "Why" - that makes business sense - can have disastrous consequences. Here's an example.

About ten years ago, a local couple opened a high-end burger restaurant (let's say it was called Burger John's) in my hometown of Springfield, Virginia. The location was dubious – across the street from a low-income apartment complex where crime was so rampant that the local police opened a small sub-station in one of the ground floor apartments.

Over the course of 3-4 months, I watched as the build-out was done, a big kitchen, filled with top-end equipment, was installed and beautiful tile flooring was laid in the dining room. Burger John's looked great – and expensive! It was an expensive franchise to buy and build, and it was going to be an expensive place to eat a burger.

The restaurant opened to a resounding thud. Every time I walked in the dining room was empty and the employees were standing around doing nothing. I inquired about the owners and was told that they were a DINK couple (Dual Income No Kids). Both worked for the Federal government in what are called SES (Senior Executive Service) positions, pulling down six-figure incomes. Why they wanted to open a restaurant was beyond me.

The employees told me that the owners came into the restaurant on weekends so I stopped by the following Saturday to introduce myself and see if I could be of some help with their marketing. They were a jovial couple in their mid-40s who insisted that all was well and business was going to pick up anytime now.

When asked why they opened the restaurant, they told a story of loving Burger John's when they both attended university in Georgia, and dreaming of someday opening a Burger John's of their own. When they heard that the company was planning on franchising, they jumped at the opportunity and, in fact, became the very first franchisees. They "didn't need" my help because every one of the company's previous locations (all adjacent to college campuses) had been an instant hit. "Marketing? Shoot, we don't even advertise!"

Within six months the restaurant was closed and, between rent, build-out, salaries, supplies, legal costs and franchise fees I estimate the couple was out somewhere between $500,000 (very conservative) and one million dollars or more. I wouldn't be surprised if they lost everything they had in their retirement savings and endured months of extreme stress all because "they always wanted to open a Burger John's."

Your "Why" not only needs to be clear, it needs to make sense, business sense. Successfully operating a small business is serious business. And if you aren't equally serious it will eat you alive.

Start With the End in Mind

When I say, "Start with the end in mind," I mean specifically that you should have a vision for selling your business at a given point in the future. If your current plan is to turn it over to your children, that's a mistake. My son, when he was about eight, said to me, "Dad, don't worry. When you're dead, I'll take over the print shop." Nice sentiment, but it didn't work out that way.

Your business will have a life cycle that will look something like this:

Startup:	Years One and Two
Growth:	Years Three Through Ten
Maturity:	Years Eleven and Beyond
Liquidity Event:	Pick Your Date

You need to keep the end in mind throughout the life cycle as well. Always be building The Book that Ray Kroc had on how to operate a profitable McDonald's. Make sure you're not taking a lot of your income "under the table" where it cannot be measured and used to support a high sale price in the future.

One reason you need to sell the business is to avoid the trap of complacency. After a long number of years – even if you're doing well financially – you will begin to lose your passion for the work. Complacency is insidious and can slowly erode your business from the inside out. Sell and move on to something new

Conclusion

This successful M Cube sequence is the key to unlock your business success:

1. Mission
2. Marketing
3. Money
4. Machine
5. Management
6. Minutiae

Unfortunately, most small business are built in this order:

1. Minutiae
2. Machine
3. Management
4. Money
5. Mission
6. Marketing

Start with your WHY, learn how to market, fund your launch and pre-profitability runway, become accounting literate, treat employees like human beings, work hard and commit to lifelong learning.

See? Easy! :-)

I hope you have been able to take away one or more pieces of actionable information from this short book. After years of planning, now that I have begun committing my thoughts on *Unlocking The M Cube* to paper, I can feel the information flowing freely from my mind through my fingers and onto the page you are reading now.

I am confident that I will be writing and sharing the subsequent chapters and books in the very near future. If you would like to connect with me, please send me a friend request on Facebook, follow me on Twitter (@frankfelker) or connect with me on LinkedIn. I also encourage you to listen to my podcast *Radio Free Enterprise*, available on the iTunes store.

Once again, here's to your success!

Frank Felker

About The Author

Frank Felker is the president of Digital Media Positioning, LLC, a content marketing and authority positioning agency in Old Town Alexandria, Virginia.

Frank is also the host of the Radio Free Enterprise podcast, available on iTunes, and creator of Radio Free Enterprise FM, the first 24/7/365 commercial-free radio station programmed specifically for entrepreneurs.

Connect with Frank on Facebook, LinkedIn or Twitter

ALEXANDRIA
VIRGINIA

www.ingramcontent.com/pod-product-compliance
Lightning Source LLC
Chambersburg PA
CBHW061206180526
45170CB00002B/984